Panama

by Meish Goldish

Consultant: Marjorie Faulstich Orellana, PhD
Professor of Urban Schooling
University of California, Los Angeles

BEARPORT PUBLISHING

New York, New York

Credits

Cover, © LifetimeStock/Shutterstock and © Photoservice/iStock; TOC, © Buteo/Shutterstock; 4, © hanohiki/Shutterstock; 5L, © GeorgePeters/iStock; 5R, © avid_creative/iStock; 7, © Gualberto Becerra/Shutterstock; 8, © GeorgePeters/iStock; 9, © Simon Dannhauer/iStock; 10T, © Ondrej Prosicky/Shutterstock; 10B, © PaaschPhotography/iStock; 11T, © Dirk Ercken/Dreamstime; 11B, © K Hanley CHDPhoto/Shutterstock; 12L, © Photoservice/iStock; 12–13, © Oyvind Martinsen/Alamy; 14T, © Werner Forman Archive/Heritage Image/AGE Fotostock; 14B, © Everett Historical/Shutterstock; 15, © Roberto Galan/iStock; 16, © Everett Historical/Shutterstock; 17, © Searagen/iStock; 18T, © revolucian/Shutterstock; 18B, © The Visual Explorer/Shutterstock; 19, © Joel Carillet/iStock; 20, © Alessandra Rusticali/Shutterstock; 21, © alantobey/iStock; 22L, © Alona Siniehina/Shutterstock; 22–23, © AS Food Studio/Shutterstock; 23R, © Anamaria Mejia/Shutterstock; 24, © Gualberto Becerra/Shutterstock; 25T, © Jonathan Mitchell/Dreamstime; 25B, © sbrogan/iStock; 26, © Ricardo Canino/Shutterstock; 27, © Mark Pitt Images/Shutterstock; 28T, © EFE News Agency/Alamy; 28B, © gladder/Shutterstock; 29, © Joel Carillet/iStock; 30T, © nimon/Shutterstock, © Yaroslaff/Shutterstock, and © JJM Stock Photography/Alamy; 30B, © sydeen/iStock; 31 (T to B), © Marianna Ianovska/Shutterstock, © K Hanley CHDPhoto/Shutterstock, © Jade Dragon/Shutterstock, © Yarr65/Shutterstock, and © Amy Nichole Harris/Shutterstock; 32, © mstraynor/Shutterstock.

Publisher: Kenn Goin
Senior Editor: Joyce Tavolacci
Creative Director: Spencer Brinker
Design: Debrah Kaiser
Photo Researcher: Thomas Persano

Library of Congress Cataloging-in-Publication Data

Names: Goldish, Meish, author.
Title: Panama / by Meish Goldish.
Description: New York, New York : Bearport Publishing, 2020. | Series:
   Countries we come from | Includes bibliographical references and index. |
   Audience: Ages 6–12.
Identifiers: LCCN 2019007201 (print) | LCCN 2019009558 (ebook) | ISBN
   9781642805772 (ebook) | ISBN 9781642805239 (library)
Subjects: LCSH: Panama—Juvenile literature.
Classification: LCC F1563.2 (ebook) | LCC F1563.2 .G65 2020 (print) | DDC
   972.87—dc23
LC record available at https://lccn.loc.gov/2019007201

For more information, write to Bearport Publishing Company, Inc., 45 West 21st Street, Suite 3B, New York, New York 10010. Printed in the United States of America.

10 9 8 7 6 5 4 3 2 1

Contents

MODERN

Amazing

Alive

Panama is a small country in Central America.

It's located on an **isthmus**.

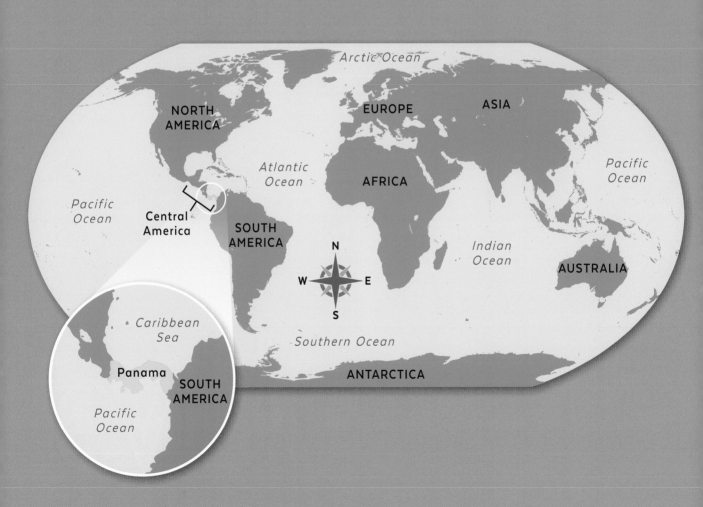

Panama connects North and South America. About four million people live in the country.

The country has mountains, rain forests, and beaches.

Rain forests cover over half of Panama.

Hundreds of rivers crisscross the land.

Along its coasts, Panama has white sand beaches. The country also has 1,500 islands!

Panama has wonderful wildlife.

Colorful toucans fly in the forests.

Furry monkeys live in the treetops.

Brightly colored frogs rest on leaves.

Panamanian golden frogs are found only in Panama. Sadly, they may now be **extinct** in the wild.

Panama City is the largest city in the country.

It's also Panama's **capital**.

About 1.5 million people live there.

Panama City has
its own rain forest!
No other capital in
the world has one.

People began living in Panama thousands of years ago.

In the 1500s, Spain took control of the land.

Later, Colombia ruled the country.

an ancient dish found in Panama

Christopher Columbus explored Panama in 1502. He was working for Spain at the time.

Panama became **independent** in 1903.

Between 1904 and 1914, the United States built a huge canal in Panama.

75,000 workers built the Panama Canal.

This waterway connects the Atlantic and Pacific oceans.

The shortcut saves ships lots of travel time.

Over 10,000 boats use the canal each year! Today, Panama controls the canal.

17

Panamanians have many jobs.

Some guide ships at the Panama Canal.

a Panama Canal worker

a construction worker

In cities, many people work in construction.

18

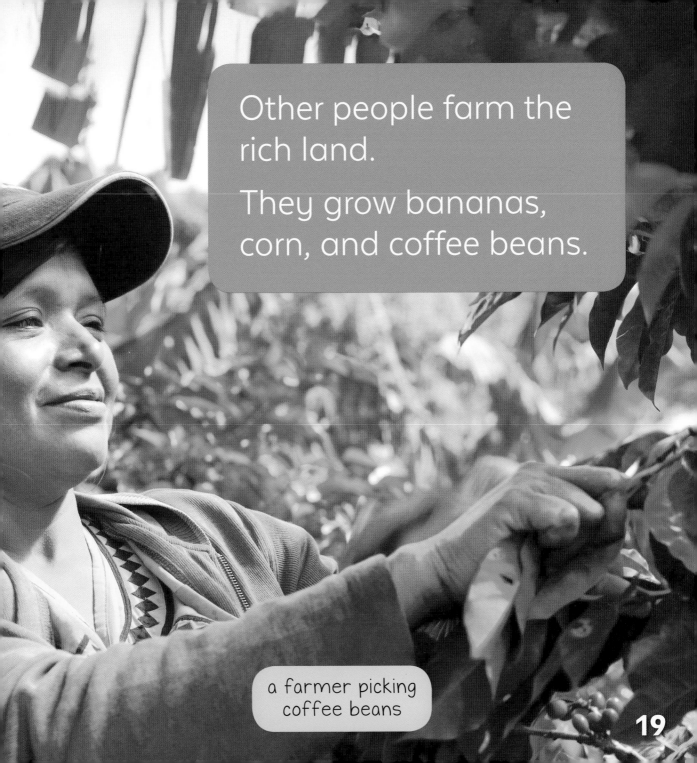

Other people farm the rich land.

They grow bananas, corn, and coffee beans.

a farmer picking coffee beans

In Panama, most people speak Spanish.

This is how you say *good morning* in Spanish:

Buenos dias
(BWAY-nohs DEE-ahs)

This is how you say *good evening*:

Buenos noches
(BWAY-nohs NOH-chess)

There are at least seven **native** groups in Panama. They speak many different languages.

A favorite dish in Panama is *sancocho* (sahn-KOH-choh).

It's chicken soup with vegetables.

Yum!

For dessert, Panamanians love sweet *bienmesabe* (bee-en-may-SAH-bay). It means "tastes good to me!"

Another popular food is shredded beef with rice and banana-like plantains.

plantains

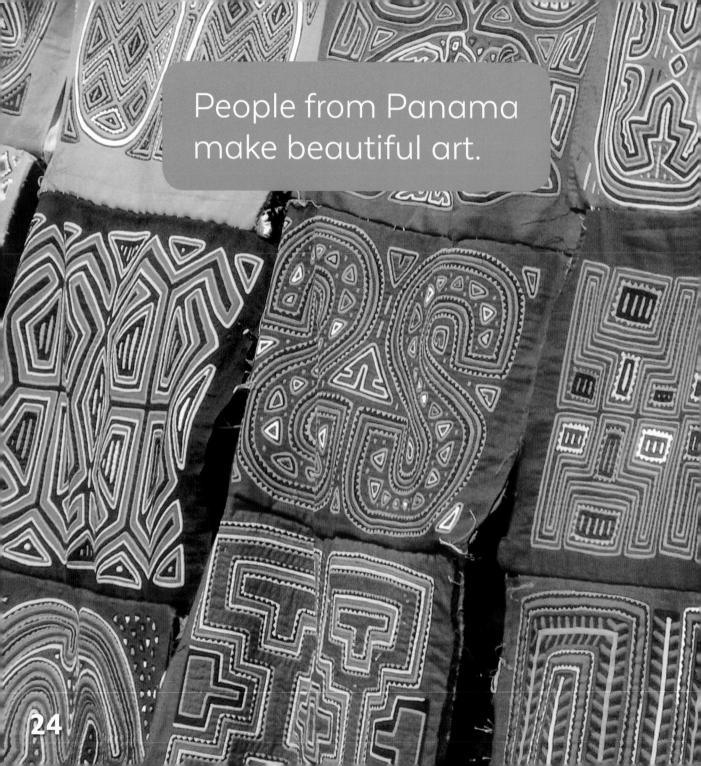

People from Panama make beautiful art.

Some native women sew *molas* (MOH-lahs).

These are made from colorful cloth.

The molas are often worn on shirts.

mola

Panamanians also carve wood and weave baskets. The baskets are made from rain forest plants.

It's *Carnaval* in Panama!

The celebration takes place in spring.

People wear wild costumes.

They sing and dance in the streets!

In November, Panamanians celebrate two Independence Days. The days mark their freedom from Spain and Colombia.

What sport do people in Panama love?

Baseball!

Other popular sports are soccer and boxing.

Surfing is also popular in Panama. Some people surf with their dogs!

Fast Facts

Capital city:
Panama City

Population of Panama:
About four million

Main language:
Spanish

Money: Balboa and
U.S. dollar

Major religion: Catholic

Neighboring countries include:
Colombia and Costa Rica

Cool Fact: In Panama, you can watch the sun rise on the Pacific Ocean and set on the Caribbean Sea!

capital (KAP-uh-tuhl) the city where a country's government is based

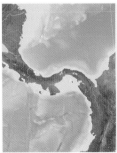

extinct (ek-STINGKT) when a kind of plant or animal has died out completely

independent (in-duh-PEN-dunt) free from outside control

isthmus (IS-muhs) a narrow strip of land with sea on either side that connects two larger land masses

native (NAY-tiv) belonging to a particular place

Glossary

Index

Read More

Adamson, Heather. *Panama (Exploring Countries).* Minneapolis, MN: Bellwether (2016).

Miller, Heather. *The Panama Canal (A Great Idea).* Chicago: Norwood House (2014).

Learn More Online

To learn more about Panama, visit
www.bearportpublishing.com/CountriesWeComeFrom

About the Author

Meish Goldish lives in New York. He has written over 300 books for children. One of his best friends is from Panama.